WHERE DOES RAIN, SLEET AND SNOW COME FROM?

Weather for Kids
(Preschool & Big Children Guide)

BABY PROFESSOR

EDUCATION KIDS

Speedy Publishing LLC
40 E. Main St. #1156
Newark, DE 19711
www.speedypublishing.com

Weather
is what is
happening in
the atmosphere—
the air around us and
the sky above us. It is
changing all the time, making
every place on earth sunny or
rainy, foggy or clear.

Weather often
controls how,
where, what
we do and
what we wear
and eat.

We talk about
the weather
in different
ways.

Different types
of weather
are sunny,
cloudy, rainy,
windy and
snowy.

The weather term "precipitation" describes the liquid and solid water particles that fall from clouds and reach the ground.

These
particles
include
rain, snow,
hail, sleet
and dew.

RAIN

Rain comes
when warm
air rises
and meets
the colder
air water
in clouds.
Where warm
and cold
meet, water
droplets form.

Rain falls from clouds in the sky in the form of water droplets.

Rain makes
the grass
green and it
makes your
garden and
the forests
grow. It
provides the
water we
drink.

Rain is an important part of the water cycle.

SLEET

Sleet is a mix of snow and raindrops that freeze on their way down from the clouds.

Sleet is partly frozen rain. Different from snow, the raindrops pass through a liquid form before freezing. The result is that they are not light and fluffy.

SNOW

During the
winter when
temperatures
are cold,
snow will fall
instead of
rain.

Snow forms when water vapor in the atmosphere freezes and turns to ice crystals.

Snow starts
off in the
same way as
rain, with tiny
droplets of
water joining
together in
clouds until
they are too
heavy.

Light and fluffy snow is often called 'powder', but it is still frozen water.

There is more to know about rain, sleet and snow. Research more and have fun!

Visit
BABY PROFESSOR
EDUCATION KIDS
www.BabyProfessorBooks.com
to download Free Baby Professor eBooks
and view our catalog of new and exciting
Children's Books